P9-CBZ-493

In Ancient Egypt

PHILIP

SAUVAIN

ILLUSTRATIONS BY

RICHARD HOOK

New

Discovery

B·O·O·K·S

New York

Maxwell Macmillan Canada
Toronto

Maxwell Macmillan International
New York • Oxford • Singapore • Sydney

First American publication 1993 by New Discovery Books, Macmillan Publishing
Company, 866 Third Avenue, New York, NY 10022
Maxwell Macmillan Canada Inc., 1200 Eglinton Avenue East, Suite 200, Don Mills,
Ontario M3C 3N1

Macmillan Publishing Company is part of the Maxwell Communication Group of
Companies

First published in Great Britain by Zoë Books Limited, 15 Worthy Lane, Winchester,
Hampshire SO23 7AB

A ZOË BOOK

Copyright © 1993 Zoë Books Limited

Devised and produced by
Zoë Books Limited
15 Worthy Lane
Winchester
Hampshire SO23 7AB
England

All rights reserved. No part of this book may be reproduced or transmitted in any form
or by any means, electronic or mechanical, including photocopying, recording, or by
any information storage and retrieval system, without permission in writing from the
publisher.

Printed in Italy by Grafedit SpA
Design: Julian Holland Publishing Ltd.
Picture research: Victoria Sturgess
Illustrations: Richard Hook
Production: Grahame Griffiths

10 9 8 7 6 5 4 3 2 1

Library of Congress Cataloging-in-Publication Data
Sauvain, Philip Arthur.
    Over 3,000 years ago : in ancient Egypt/Philip Sauvain.
      p. cm. — (History detective)
    Includes index.
    Summary: Describes what life was like in ancient Egypt, discussing such aspects as
farming, government, trading, architecture, and religion and beliefs.
      ISBN 0-02-781084-4
    1. Egypt—Civilization—To 332 B.C.—Juvenile literature. (1. Egypt—Civilization—
To 332 B.C.) I. Title. II. Series.
DT61.S277   1993
932—dc20   92-43031

Photographic acknowledgments

The publishers wish to acknowledge, with thanks, the following photographic sources:

7,11 Ancient Art and Architecture Collection; 15 Bolton Museum and Art Gallery
(model made by Mr. H. Ewings of Bury); 19,23 Ancient Art and Architecture Collection;
27 School of Archaeology, Classics and Oriental Studies, University of Liverpool

Cover inset Tony Stone Photolibrary, London

CONTENTS

One of the world's greatest civilizations began to grow up along the Nile River about 5,000 years ago. The long, thin river valley was the land of the Egyptians. For almost 3,000 years they built towns and cities and huge temples and pyramids. People who visited Egypt from other lands were impressed by what they saw. The Egyptians were ruled by kings and sometimes by queens. They believed that these pharaohs were living gods.

The main reason why people lived in this valley was because the Nile gave them the water they needed to grow food in the hot desert. The Egyptians owed many other things to the Nile as well. They hunted the fish, birds, and animals that lived in the marshes and in the river. They used the papyrus reeds to make paper, rope, and baskets. They also used the river for travel and transportation. The Egyptians were the first people to use sailing boats. The Nile was always busy with shipping. Over 4,600 years ago Egyptian sailors took boats like these out into the open waters of the Mediterranean Sea. They took with them goods such as cloth and papyrus, which they sold to people in nearby lands.

Ruled by the pharaohs

The rule of the pharaohs began between about 4,200 and 4,700 years ago. They lived in Lower Egypt, in the flat lowlands of the delta region. Here the course of the Nile divides into a number of waterways before entering the sea. The pharaohs built their capital at Memphis, close to the site of modern Cairo. They also built great pyramids as burial places for themselves and their families.

The pharaohs who came after them built a new capital far to the south, much farther up the river in Upper Egypt. It was called Thebes. Between 3,000 and 3,600 years ago great temples were built at Karnak, Luxor, and Abu Simbel. Instead of building pyramids as burial places, the pharaohs had splendid tombs carved out for themselves in a dry, rocky valley. This site is called the Valley of the Kings.

The Egyptians were able to build a great civilization here because of the river. The Nile flooded over its banks each year. When the waters went down, they left behind a layer of mud. Crops grew well in this black fertile soil. They ripened in the hot desert sun and were watered from the Nile. As a result, the farmers of Egypt were able to grow much more food than they needed for themselves. The extra amount was used to feed the people who did other jobs.

The shadoof was used to take water from the river to the fields. It was simple to use and made light work of a very tiring job.

River birds such as wild ducks and geese lived among the reeds of the Nile. Rich Egyptians hunted them for sport. They used a hunting stick. This piece of wood was rather like the boomerang used by people in Australia. It was shaped so that it could be thrown quickly at a moving target.

There were skilled workers who made tools, clothes, pottery, ornaments, and jewelry. There were soldiers, priests in the temples, and royal officials. They were paid wages by the pharaoh, who raised the money from the taxes that people had to pay.

Some royal officials were paid to organize irrigation, the watering of the crops. In the dry season, farmers used a shadoof. This machine was used to lift buckets of water from the Nile. A weight at one end of the pole balanced the bucket of water at the other. This made it easy to swivel the bucket around. It was then emptied into the irrigation canal, the ditch that carried water to the fields.

We shall probably never see a complete Egyptian boat. The wood they were made of has long since rotted away. However, we do know what the boats looked like. This is because the Egyptians left small model boats in the burial places of their pharaohs. Each boat had a single mast for its large sail. It was steered by a long oar.

HISTORY DETECTIVE

Long ago, people used to move their boats through the water by using paddles or oars. Sometimes they stuck a long pole in the riverbed and pushed the boat along. It was the Egyptians who first made sails. These caught the wind and carried the boat forward. Rowers were still needed on calm days.

The Egyptians believed that their pharaoh, the god-king, would live forever after he had died. They buried him in a great tomb made of stone. This was built to last for all time. Over 4,500 years ago the tombs were built deep inside vast pyramids made from thousands of stone blocks. The pharaoh made sure of this himself. He ordered work to begin on his own pyramid as soon as he became pharaoh. The first of the great pyramids was built for King Zoser at Saqqara, about 4,680 years ago. Zoser's pyramid had huge steps. The Egyptians believed that after death the pharaoh became a sun-god. He would need the steps so that he could climb up to the sun.

Zoser's pyramid was built by a famous architect named Imhotep. Beneath the pyramid was a group of burial chambers. Here the pharaoh and the members of his family were buried with all the possessions they would need for their life after death. Afterward the entrance was closed off with huge slabs of stone, to keep thieves from stealing the valuable jewels and ornaments inside.

The most famous pyramid was at Giza. The Great Pyramid there was built for the pharaoh Cheops about 4,560 years ago. It can still be seen today. It stands 481 feet (147 meters) high. Its four sides, each 758 feet (231 meters) long, make up a perfect square.

9

Even though the Great Pyramid of Cheops is over 4,500 years old, it is still the biggest stone building in the world. More than two million stone blocks were used in its construction. Each one weighed, on average, about 2.5 tons.

Blocks of stone

Some of the stones for the Great Pyramid were cut from a quarry at Aswan, 500 miles (800 kilometers) up the Nile. Most stones, however, came from local quarries on the eastern side of the river. They were shaped in the quarry by workers using special tools. Some of the stones they cut still have markings on them that told the workmen on the site what to do. One block of stone is marked with a sign meaning "this side up," just like a modern packing case! When the stones were ready, they were dragged to the water's edge and carried across the Nile on barges. At Giza they were fitted together like the pieces in a giant jigsaw puzzle.

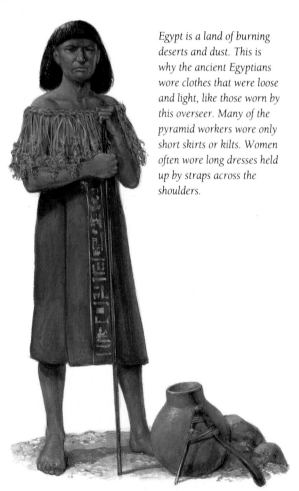

Egypt is a land of burning deserts and dust. This is why the ancient Egyptians wore clothes that were loose and light, like those worn by this overseer. Many of the pyramid workers wore only short skirts or kilts. Women often wore long dresses held up by straps across the shoulders.

Without using a compass, workers built the pyramids so that the four sides faced exactly north, south, east, and west. Even though the Great Pyramid is twice as long as a football field, its four sides vary in length by no more than 8 inches (20 centimeters) — about the length of a pencil! An even bigger problem was making sure that the great building site was level to start with. Modern experts were amazed to find that even though it covers an area of 13 acres (5.3 hectares), the base of the pyramid is level to within about half an inch (1.75 centimeters). Other pharaohs built pyramids nearly as big as the one erected by Cheops. These pyramids were guarded by a huge statue, which had the head of a human and the body of a lion. This Sphinx still stands today.

Many thousands of workers were needed to build the pyramids. An ancient Greek writer named Herodotus said that 10,000 men worked in gangs to build them. Modern experts think that fewer workers were needed. Even so, it took a team of many men to pull just one of the heavy stone blocks into place. They put wooden logs under the blocks as rollers, to make it easier to move them over the ground. They also built raised sloping paths, or ramps. The stones were dragged up these ramps to the sides of the pyramid as it was being built.

Archaeologists are people who study ancient ruins and remains. They find out how people lived long ago. The colossal size of the pyramids tells them that the pharaohs were good at organizing people to do work. The accuracy with which the pyramids were built tells them that the Egyptians were also good at mathematics and science. The burial chambers in the pyramids and the Valley of the Kings help them to know more about ancient religious beliefs.

HISTORY DETECTIVE

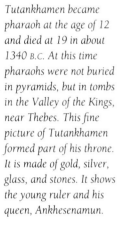

Tutankhamen became pharaoh at the age of 12 and died at 19 in about 1340 B.C. At this time pharaohs were not buried in pyramids, but in tombs in the Valley of the Kings, near Thebes. This fine picture of Tutankhamen formed part of his throne. It is made of gold, silver, glass, and stones. It shows the young ruler and his queen, Ankhesenamun.

Rich nobles built their villas and farmhouses on the banks of the Nile River. As most of the country was harsh desert, the farms by the river's edge had many advantages. In most years the hot climate, river water, and rich soil produced good harvests of grain. The hard work in the fields was done by the peasants. They toiled in the orchards and vineyards of the nobles. They looked after the cattle, sheep, and goats. The farming year was organized according to the Nile floods. These happened each year between the months of June and September. The floodwater traveled to Egypt from the mountain streams of Central Africa, thousands of miles to the south. As the river rose higher and higher, muddy water spilled over into the surrounding fields.

The farmers welcomed the floods, which made the soil moist and left behind a thin layer of fertile mud. Since the peasants could not work in water-covered fields, they worked on other projects at this time, such as building the great temples and tombs. When the water level started to fall in October, however, the peasants were needed on the land again. They built walls of mud to hold back the floodwater. The next job was to dig the soil with plows. Wheat and barley were sown by hand. Sheep were then driven onto the soil, so that they would tread in the seeds firmly with their feet. As the crops grew, laborers worked at the shadoof, making sure that water continued to flow along the irrigation ditches to the fields. The water gave the roots of the crops the moisture they needed.

In the Nile Valley grain was harvested in the spring. The ripe ears of wheat were held with one hand. The other hand held a sharp stone sickle. This was used to cut the stalks below.

Harvest time

By the end of February the land was no longer moist after the great floods. For three months it became drier and drier. It was now the season for harvesting the ripened grain. The peasants made sure that they harvested it long before the Nile flooded the fields once more. In some years the river let them down and failed to flood. Then the crops would not grow. There was a famine. The people starved because there was no wheat to make bread.

During their long history the Egyptians used new tools and methods to grow their crops. They first used oxen to pull a wooden plow about 5,000 years ago. These strong male cattle were used to do work on the farm. When the wheat and barley were being harvested, the farmers used sickles to cut the crop. These were sharp stone tools. Their cutting edge was curved, which made them easier to use. The peasants collected the crop in baskets made of papyrus and took it to the farmhouse.

After the grape juice in the vats had stood for a long time, it began to bubble and change into wine. The ancient Egyptians kept wine in tall pottery jars. The date when the wine was made was written on each jar.

We know that Egyptian villas had flat roofs and thick walls because models of farmhouses have been found in the tombs of kings and rich nobles. The roofs did not slope because rain was rare in Egypt. The thick walls kept the rooms cool inside.

The crops were laid out on stone floors and then threshed with sticks. Threshing made the ears of wheat, which contain the grain, separate from the stalks. When the grain was tossed in the air, the lighter husks and bits of straw were separated out. Grindstones were used to make flour. The ancient Egyptians grew other crops as well as wheat and barley. Flax was grown to make linen cloth. Egyptians also grew vegetables and fruit. Fig, date, olive, and pomegranate trees shaded villas from the sun. Vineyards provided large black or purple grapes that were made into wine. The workers emptied them into stone vats and stamped on the grapes to make the juice run out. They held onto ropes as they did so and chanted in time to a song.

Genesis, the first book of the Bible, tells us the story of Joseph's journey into Egypt. It gives us a number of clues about farming in the Nile Valley more than 3,000 years ago. We read how the Egyptians kept fat cattle and grew wheat with ears "full and good" and also "ripe grapes." In years of famine, however, the cattle were lean, and the wheat was "withered, thin, and blasted with the east wind." That was why Joseph advised the pharaoh of Egypt to stock up any extra wheat grown in the good years in buildings called granaries. Then, if the crops failed in a bad year, the surplus grain could be taken out of these grain supplies and used to feed the people in the "years of famine" that followed.

HISTORY DETECTIVE

Rich Egyptian farmers and nobles had many slaves and servants to look after their everyday needs. Egyptian paintings show attendants pouring warm or cold water from a vase over the master or mistress of the house. Afterward they covered them with sweet-smelling oils and perfumes.

Women servants can be seen helping the ladies of the house dress and put garlands of flowers in their hair. Young slave girls wave large fans to send cool breezes through the rooms of the villa. Servants use fly whisks to get rid of tiresome desert insects. Objects in the tombs of the pharaohs show that many of the things we use today were known to the Egyptians over 3,000 years ago. They used lipstick, hand mirrors and combs, gold rings and necklaces.

Houses were furnished with fine couches, tables, and chairs. Some of these have also been discovered in the Valley of the Kings, preserved in the dry desert air.

Rich Egyptians liked to entertain guests. As you can see, when they held banquets, they employed entertainers to amuse the guests. Musicians played the drums, harp, and flute. There were even instruments with strings like the modern guitar. Dancers clapped their hands in time to the rhythm. Clowns made the guests laugh. Wrestlers and jugglers put on shows of strength and skill.

A life of luxury

Not all villas were built on the banks of the Nile. Many rich Egyptians lived in the towns. There they built their homes facing shady avenues or narrow streets. Most were made of bricks of dried mud and built so that the main rooms faced north. This kept them away from the burning rays of the sun at midday. Also facing north was the veranda. This room, with its flat roof and tall pillars, was open to the cool night breezes.

The more luxurious homes were separated from each other by large gardens. These were filled with flowers and with trees that gave shade to the house. Some owners built a pool where they kept fish. In another part of the garden they built rooms where the servants and slaves worked and slept. The kitchens were also built here, well away from the house. Sometimes small temples, where all the family could worship, were built in the garden as well.

This beautiful chair was one of a number found in the tomb of Tutankhamen. Some were carved from a wood called cedar of Lebanon or Cilician fir. One was a small chair made for Tutankhamen when he was a little boy. It was made of ivory and a hard, black wood called ebony. The young pharaoh was buried with many prized possessions.

This female acrobat with her long hair would have entertained the nobles as they wined and dined. There were dancing girls and musicians. Servants went from guest to guest, bringing them food and drink. We know such scenes happened because they were painted on the walls of sealed tombs. Many wall paintings have survived in the Valley of the Kings and the nearby Valley of the Queens.

The tables at an Egyptian banquet were laden with food. Meat dishes included beef, fish, goose, and duck, flavored with onions and garlic. Fresh bread, honey, cakes, and pastries were eaten with figs and dates. Drinks included beer and wine.

Inside the house colorful cloths covered the walls. The rooms were furnished with stools, folding beds, couches, folding chairs, and square tables. Many of these were beautifully carved with figures and animals and decorated with precious metals and pieces of colored glass and pottery.

Most of the villas of the rich had bathrooms with running water and a toilet. People entertained their guests in a large downstairs room. The women and children of the house had their own private living rooms upstairs. This was where the children played with their toys. Even these seem very modern when we look at them today. Dolls sometimes had arms and legs that could be moved by pulling strings.

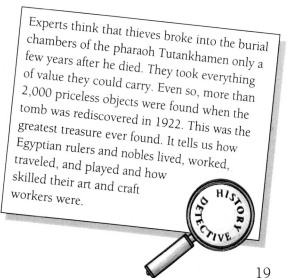

Experts think that thieves broke into the burial chambers of the pharaoh Tutankhamen only a few years after he died. They took everything of value they could carry. Even so, more than 2,000 priceless objects were found when the tomb was rediscovered in 1922. This was the greatest treasure ever found. It tells us how Egyptian rulers and nobles lived, worked, traveled, and played and how skilled their art and craft workers were.

RELIGION AND BELIEFS

The great stone gods of ancient Egypt still stare out across the desert and the waters of the Nile. Tourists fly past Abu Simbel or sail down the Nile to Luxor, near ancient Thebes. They descend into the tombs of the pharaohs in the Valley of the Kings. Entering this cool, dark world, it is easy to imagine a funeral procession over 3,000 years ago.

When a pharaoh like Tutankhamen died, his body would be handed over to the embalmers. They used special ointments to preserve the body and wound bandages around it tightly. After ten weeks this mummy was ready. It was placed inside a large wooden coffin. This was shaped like the mummy, with a carved and painted head showing the face of the dead pharaoh.

The mummy was carried in procession by the priests. In the temple they sacrificed animals as an offering to the gods. The priests were followed by the mourners, who carried the dead man's most treasured possessions. These were put in the burial chamber next to the pharaoh's body, for use on his long journey to the other world.

A religious life

The ancient Egyptians worshiped many gods. About 3,350 years ago a pharaoh named Akhenaton tried to make people worship one god only. This was Aton, the sun-god. When Akhenaton died, the people once more went back to their old beliefs in many gods.

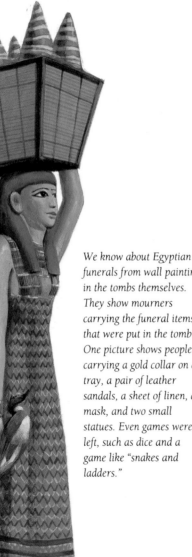

We know about Egyptian funerals from wall paintings in the tombs themselves. They show mourners carrying the funeral items that were put in the tomb. One picture shows people carrying a gold collar on a tray, a pair of leather sandals, a sheet of linen, a mask, and two small statues. Even games were left, such as dice and a game like "snakes and ladders."

In order to make a mummy, the embalmers first removed the parts of the body that would decay. They left the skin and bones. These were dried out by covering them with salt. Then the body was wrapped in bandages that were moistened with gum and ointment so that they would stick together. Finally the mummy was placed in a body-shaped coffin made of wood.

Worshiping the gods formed a part of everyday life. The Egyptians believed that many animals were sacred, too. In pictures their gods were often shown with animal heads. The god Anubis had the doglike head of a jackal and Horus the hooked beak of a falcon. The goddess Bast had the head of a cat. The priests were in charge of the rituals in the temples. They shaved their heads and eyebrows and bathed their bodies several times a day to make sure they were clean and pure.

The Egyptians believed there was life after death for everyone, not just the pharaohs. Those who could afford it paid an embalmer to preserve the body of a relative who died. They were offered various types of embalming, ranging from the cheap to the expensive. Even some sacred animals, such as crocodiles and cats, were made into mummies and buried in special graveyards.

When people were buried, they were left with their favorite possessions and provided with supplies of food and drink for the journey after death. That is why gold ornaments, jewelry, weapons, models of shops and other buildings, and small statues of the gods have been found in some of the tombs. Archaeologists call objects like these funeral goods. Poor people, too, were often buried with their few possessions such as a cheap bead necklace or a single dagger. They could not afford embalming or grand tombs and were buried in shallow graves.

In the 1960s the people of modern Egypt had a problem. The huge temple at Abu Simbel, with its giant statues, stood in the way of a new dam being built across the Nile near the town of Aswan. When the dam was built, the rise in water level would drown the temple for good. Experts were sent to Egypt by the United Nations. They planned to move the temple to higher ground. Each part of the temple was cut out from the rock, piece by piece, and put together again higher up. In this way one of the greatest Egyptian temples was saved. By studying it we can learn more about the ancient Egyptians and their gods.

HISTORY DETECTIVE

The temple at Abu Simbel was built for the pharaoh Ramses II about 3,250 years ago. Today its huge statues have been rebuilt high above Lake Nasser, which now fills the flooded valley of the Nile.

Although many Egyptian towns were built well over 3,000 years ago, we know quite a lot about them. For instance, the town of El-Amarna was built by the pharaoh Akhenaton about 3,350 years ago. Not long after the pharaoh died, the Egyptians left the new town. When archaeologists discovered the deserted ruins of the town thousands of years later, they were able to work out what it looked like when it was new. They found that it had three main streets. These separated El-Amarna into three main parts. In one area were the pharaoh's palaces and temples built in honor of the sun-god Aton. In another area houses of brick were built for the officials and merchants of the town.

In the third area were the offices of the pharaoh's officials and craft workshops. Here you could have seen skilled workers making pottery, bricks, jewelry, ornaments, and goods made from leather, metals, and wood. Stores and markets were found here as well.

These markets included meat stores. We know what they looked like because models and wall paintings of them have been found in Egyptian burial chambers. They show slabs of meat hanging down from the ceiling of a butcher's shop and workers making bread in a bakery.

Taxes and scribes

The Egyptians were among the first people in the world to build towns as well as villages. Each town was surrounded by a wall so that it could be easily defended. Almost all the Egyptian towns, such as Thebes and Giza, were built on or close to the banks of the Nile. They grew up as places where people could easily meet to do business. Farmers, merchants, and craft workers sold or exchanged goods in the town markets.

The towns were also good places from which rulers could govern the people and collect taxes. The pharaoh made everyone pay something toward the cost of keeping his soldiers, priests, and officials. The gold and silver paid by the public were taken by the tax collectors. A clerk called a scribe wrote down the amount each person paid. The scribes used pen and ink to write on paper. Our word "paper" comes from papyrus, the kind of reed first used for making paper in ancient Egypt.

Scribes sat next to the tax collectors in the center of the town. They recorded details of the amount of silver or gold that each person paid as taxes to the pharaoh.

The potter used a wheel to make pottery. As he spun the wheel around, he used his hands to shape the lump of wet clay in the middle into a smooth, round pot or vase.

Models and wall paintings show us life in the busy stores and markets of ancient Egyptian towns. Here a baker kneads dough into a loaf of bread.

The Egyptians were one of the earliest peoples to have a language they could write down instead of just speaking to one another. They invented a way of drawing pictures to represent words. These symbols are called hieroglyphs. A bird represented the sound *wr* and a mouth the sound *r*. Together the two symbols made up a word meaning "great." Hieroglyphs were often carved in wood and stone. A simpler version of the script was used for writing quickly on paper.

It is rare for an archaeologist to find an unbroken pot from long ago. Instead, these experts usually have to piece together the bits of pot they find buried in the earth. They work out how to fit them together, using the lines, patterns, and colors on the pots as clues. Often there are pots in other museums that help experts know what their own pots should look like when complete. Then they glue the fragments together to make a complete pot.

HISTORY DETECTIVE

B.C.	(before the birth of Christ)
4200	The first Egyptians build huts along the banks of the Nile River
3300	The Egyptians begin to use sailing boats on the Nile
3250	The Egyptians learn how to use copper to make knives and tools
3100	The Egyptians invent hieroglyphic writing to write down words and messages
3000	The Egyptians begin to use oxen to pull their plows. Egyptian priests calculate that each year has 365 days.
2700	The start of the Old Kingdom. At this time the pharaohs lived in Lower (northern) Egypt.
2686	The architect Imhotep builds the stepped pyramid at Saqqara for the pharaoh Zoser
2648	Death of Zoser
2575	The Great Pyramid at Giza is built by the pharaoh Cheops
2566	Death of Cheops
2550	The pharaoh Chephren builds a pyramid at Giza. The Sphinx bears his head on the body of a lion.
2533	Death of Chephren
2200	End of the Old Kingdom
2000	Start of the Middle Kingdom. The pharaohs move their capital from Memphis to Thebes in Upper (southern) Egypt.

1800	End of the Middle Kingdom
1650	The Egyptians begin to use bronze, a mixture of copper and tin
1600	The Egyptians begin to use horsedrawn chariots. Start of the New Kingdom. The pharaohs build great temples and are buried in the Valley of the Kings.
1488	Queen Hatshepsut rules as pharaoh for 20 years. As a badge of her authority she wears men's clothes and a false beard.
1363	Akhenaton urges the Egyptians to worship one god, Aton, instead of many gods
1360	Death of Akhenaton
1339	Death of the young pharaoh Tutankhamen
1270	Ramses II builds the great temple at Abu Simbel
1237	Death of Ramses II
1235	The Israelite tribes leave Egypt. Their story is described in the Bible, in the book of Exodus.
1090	The end of the New Kingdom

Abu Simbel: the site of a great temple built by Ramses II on a bank of the Nile River. It was moved to another site in 1968 when the Aswan High Dam was built.

Akhenaton: a pharaoh who ruled Egypt more than 3,350 years ago

archaeologist: a scientist who studies the relics and ruins left behind by ancient peoples

Aswan: a town in southern Egypt, built opposite an island in the Nile. Today it is the site of two great dams.

Aton: the sun-god worshiped during the reign of Akhenaton

burial chamber: a stone-sided tomb, usually built underground

Cheops: a pharaoh who died in 2566 B.C. He was buried under the Great Pyramid at Giza.

delta: a region where a river divides and spills over a flat plain before it enters the sea

El-Amarna: a town in central Egypt built by the pharaoh Akhenaton

embalmer: a person who preserves dead bodies by treating them with ointments

famine: a time when people are starving, often because their crops have failed to grow

fertile soil: a soil that is rich in the foods that help plants to grow

flax: a crop grown for its stalks, which are beaten and turned into thread. This is woven into cloth called linen.

funeral goods: objects placed in the graves of dead people when they are buried

Giza: the site of the Great Pyramid and the Sphinx, on the outskirts of modern Cairo

granary: a building used to store grain and keep it dry

grindstone: a rough stone used for sharpening knives or for milling flour

hieroglyph: a system of picture symbols used as a form of writing

Imhotep: an Egyptian doctor and architect who lived about 4,680 years ago. He designed the stepped pyramid at Saqqara.

irrigation: a way of taking water from a river, lake, or well and carrying it to fields so that crops can be grown

mourner: somebody showing public grief for a dead person

mummy: the preserved body of a dead person or animal. Mummies were made in ancient Peru as well as in Egypt.

papyrus: a type of reed that grows in the Nile River, or the paper made from it

peasant: a poor person who lives in the countryside and works on the land

pharaoh: a ruler of ancient Egypt, believed to be a god

pomegranate: a fruit with a tough skin and sweet flesh full of seeds

pyramid: a massive stone building with a square base and four triangular sides

ramp: an artificial slope. The builders of the pyramids raised ramps to bring stones to the higher levels. The ramps were taken away when the building was finished.

ritual: a religious ceremony

sacrifice: to make an offering to the gods by killing an animal

scribe: someone whose job is to write things out by hand or to keep written records

shadoof: a simple machine used to raise buckets of water from the Nile River for irrigation

sickle: a farm tool with a short handle and a curved blade, used to cut long grass or wheat

Sphinx: a statue of a human being with an animal's body. The Sphinx at Giza is thought to represent the head of the pharaoh Chephren on a lion's body.

taxes: fees or goods that the people have to pay or give to the government, to provide public services

thresh: to separate grain from the stalk by beating

vat: a large tub made of wood or stone in which wine is made or other drinks are stored

veranda: a cool gallery or porch, open to the air and providing shade

villa: a house or a farm built in the countryside by wealthy people

vineyard: farmland where grapes are grown to make wine

Zoser: An Egyptian pharaoh who died in 2648 B.C.

For Further Reading

Bendick, Jeanne. *Egyptian Tombs*. New York: Franklin Watts, 1989.

Cohen, Daniel. *Ancient Egypt*. New York: Doubleday, 1990.

Diamond, Arthur. *Egypt: Gift of the Nile*. New York: Dillon Press, 1992.

Fleming, Stuart. *The Egyptians*. New York: New Discovery Books, 1992.

Giblin, James Cross. *The Riddle of the Rosetta Stone: Key to Ancient Egypt*. New York: HarperCollins, 1990.

Gold, Susan Dudley. *The Pharaohs' Curse*. New York: Crestwood House, 1990.

Kerr, James. *Egyptian Farmers*. New York: Franklin Watts, 1991.

Morley, Jacqueline. *An Egyptian Pyramid: Inside Story*. New York: Peter Bedrick Books, 1991.

Odisk, Pamela. *The Egyptians*. Englewood Cliffs, NJ: Silver Burdett Press, 1989.

Venturo, Piero. *Journey to Egypt*. New York: Viking, 1986.

Woods, Geraldine. *Science in Ancient Egypt*. New York: Franklin Watts, 1988.

INDEX